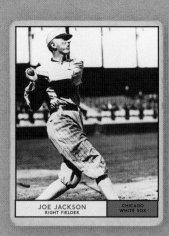

JOE JACKSON
RIGHT FIELDER

CHICAGO
WHITE SOX

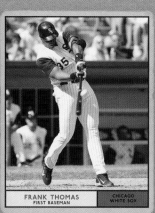

FRANK THOMAS
FIRST BASEMAN

CHICAGO
WHITE SOX

THE STORY OF THE CHICAGO WHITE SOX

Published by Creative Education
P.O. Box 227, Mankato, Minnesota 56002
Creative Education is an imprint of The Creative Company
www.thecreativecompany.us

Design and production by Blue Design
Art direction by Rita Marshall
Printed by Corporate Graphics in the United States of America

Photographs by Corbis (Bettmann), Getty Images (Mark Cunningham/MLB Photos, Jonathan Daniel, Focus On Sport, Otto Greule Jr, Bruce Kluckhohn/MLB Photos, Saul Loeb/AFP, Brad Mangin/MLB Photos, Jim McIsaac, Martin D. McReynolds, Francis Miller/Time & Life Pictures, National Baseball Hall of Fame Library/MLB Photos, Scott Olson, Rich Pilling/MLB Photos, Rogers Photo Archive, Mark Rucker/ Transcendental Graphics, Herb Scharfman/Sports Imagery, Donald F. Smith/Time & Life Pictures, Jamie Squire, Ron Vesely/MLB Photos)

Library of Congress Cataloging-in-Publication Data

LeBoutillier, Nate.
The story of the Chicago White Sox / by Nate LeBoutillier.
p. cm. — (Baseball: the great American game)
Includes index.
Summary: The history of the Chicago White Sox professional baseball team from its inaugural 1901 season to today, spotlighting the team's greatest players and most memorable moments.
ISBN 978-1-60818-036-3
1. Chicago White Sox (Baseball team)—History—Juvenile literature. I. Title. II. Series.

GV875.C58L43 2010
796.357'6477311—dc22   2010023568

CPSIA: 110310 PO1381

First Edition
9 8 7 6 5 4 3 2 1

Page 3: First baseman Paul Konerko
Page 4: Left fielder Juan Pierre

BASEBALL: THE GREAT AMERICAN GAME

THE STORY
OF THE
CHICAGO
WHITE SOX

Nate LeBoutillier

CREATIVE EDUCATION

CONTENTS

A HOT START

hy is Chicago, Illinois, called the "Windy City"? Maybe it's due to the city's location on the shores of Lake Michigan, where cold gusts are common. Maybe it's because of the Great Chicago Fire of 1871 that caused Chicago to be rebuilt with tall, strong buildings and wide streets that funnel the wind. Some people say it's a reference to the town's history of politicians, who have been known to flap their gums in grand speeches promising this or that. Perhaps the name is actually a misnomer—studies have shown that Chicago's average winds aren't as strong as those in cities such as Boston, Massachusetts, or Oklahoma City, Oklahoma.

Regardless, the Windy City is a good nickname, and it has been a part of Chicago for many decades, just like the White Sox professional baseball team. In 1900, a former baseball player named Charles Comiskey moved his minor-league franchise from St. Paul, Minnesota, to the Windy City to join up with the newly formed American League (AL). The White Sox became Chicago's second entry into big-time

A big city with a population passionate about its professional teams, Chicago is regarded as one of the United States' top sports markets.

PITCHER · ED WALSH

As a young man, "Big Ed" Walsh worked in a Pennsylvania coal mine, where he developed great arm and shoulder strength. He joined the big leagues with nothing but that strong arm and a fastball. On team road trips, he roomed with spitballer Elmer Stricklett, who taught Walsh his craft. Once Walsh mastered the spitball, he mastered major-league hitters—inning after inning until he overworked his arm and could pitch no more. In 1908, Walsh pitched 464 innings, a modern record. He won 40 games while throwing 42 complete games that year—both White Sox feats that have never been duplicated.

ED WALSH
PITCHER

CHICAGO
WHITE SOX

STATS

White Sox seasons: 1904–16

Height: 6-foot-1

Weight: 193

- **1.82 career ERA**
- **2,964 career innings pitched**
- **5-time AL leader in games pitched**
- **Baseball Hall of Fame inductee (1946)**

baseball, as a National League (NL) franchise that would soon be called the Cubs had already staked a claim in Chicago in 1876.

In 1901, the AL elevated itself to "major league" status, and the White Sox went 83–53 and won the very first AL title on the big-league level. The seven other charter teams of the 1901 AL included the Baltimore Orioles, Boston Americans, Cleveland Blues, Detroit Tigers, Milwaukee Brewers, Philadelphia Athletics, and Washington Senators. Chicago's home that season was the South Side Grounds, and its top star was pitcher Clark Griffith, who won 24 games on the mound and also managed the ballclub.

It wasn't until 1903 that the AL and the more-established NL started meeting at their seasons' end to have an all-out championship that came to be known as the World Series. In 1906, the White Sox, led by player/manager Fielder Jones and nicknamed "The Hitless Wonders," won the AL pennant, despite sporting the lowest

CLARK GRIFFITH

batting average (.230) in the league, and made their first appearance in the World Series. Their opponent was the crosstown Cubs, who boasted the best record in either league with a 116–36 mark.

Games 1 and 2 of the seven-game series were played amid snow flurries, and the teams split. Then the Sox handed the ball to pitcher Ed Walsh, who twirled a two-hit shutout in Game 3. The Cubs knotted the series again in Game 4 before "Big Ed" returned to earn another victory in Game 5. Game 6 was the series clincher for the White Sox, as they downed the Cubs 8–3 to capture the franchise's first World Series title. Many people consider the South-Side White Sox's victory over the North-Side Cubs one of baseball's greatest World Series upsets. The outcome was heaven for the White Sox and a bitter pill for the Cubs. "There is one thing I will never believe," said Cubs manager Frank Chance, "and that is the Sox are better than the Cubs."

CHARLES COMISKEY

Ed Walsh had a well-earned reputation as a workhorse, leading all AL hurlers in innings pitched in 1907, 1908, 1911, and 1912.

ED WALSH

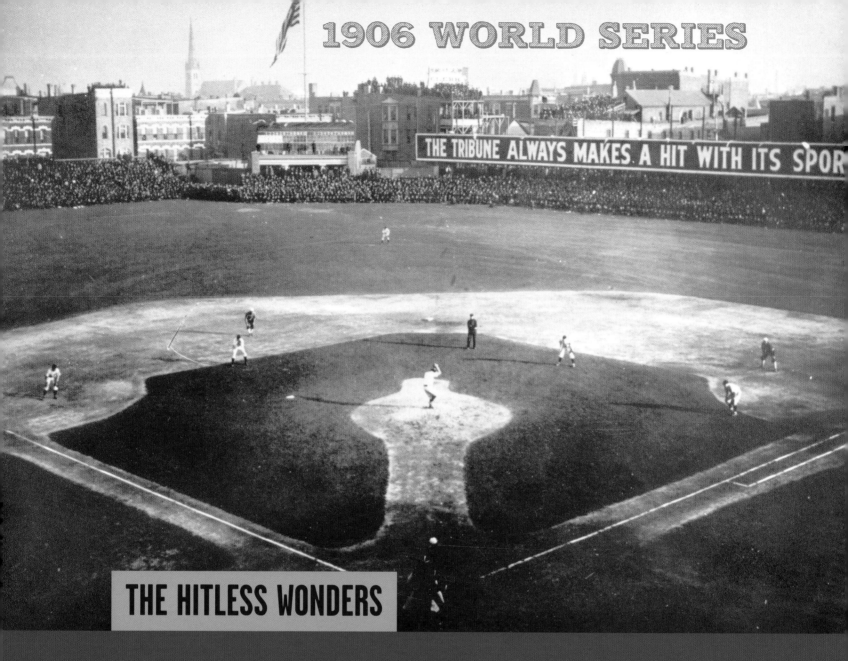

THE TRIBUNE ALWAYS MAKES A HIT WITH ITS SPOR

THE HITLESS WONDERS

WHITE SOX

When the 1906 Chicago Cubs won the NL pennant, they did it in dominating fashion, winning 116 games— the most in major-league history at the time. Across town, the Chicago White Sox earned their own pennant in the AL. But they did it in a completely different manner, seemingly despite their play. The "Hitless Wonders," as they came to be known, won 93 games that year while managing just 7 home runs and a .230 team batting average, the lowest in baseball. When the two teams faced off in the first and only all-Chicago World Series, the Cubs were heavily favored. But four

games into the best-of-seven series, despite the White Sox's having committed 6 errors and gotten only 11 hits, the teams were tied at two games apiece. And then the series really turned upside down. In the next 2 games, the White Sox sprayed 26 hits around the field, including 8 off Hall of Fame pitcher Mordecai Brown. Sox second baseman Frank Isbell hit 4 doubles in Game 5, and shortstop George Davis accounted for 10 runs in Games 5 and 6. The Hitless Wonders scored eight runs in each of those games to win the World Series and earn Chicago bragging rights.

CATCHER · CARLTON FISK

In his first game for the Chicago White Sox, Carlton "Pudge" Fisk smashed a three-run homer against his former team, the Boston Red Sox. Fisk swung an uncommonly powerful bat for a catcher and, for a time, owned the White Sox career home run record as well as the major-league home run record for catchers. But Fisk's greatest strengths were his work ethic and durability; he managed to play a record 2,226 games at baseball's most physically demanding position, despite suffering numerous leg injuries. Fisk played until he was 45, spending 13 of his 24 major-league seasons with Chicago.

CARLTON FISK
CATCHER

CHICAGO
WHITE SOX

STATS

White Sox seasons: 1981–93

Height: 6-foot-2

Weight: 220

- **1972 AL Rookie of the Year**

- **376 career HR**

- **11-time All-Star**

- **Baseball Hall of Fame inductee (2000)**

FIRST BASEMAN · FRANK THOMAS

Frank Thomas led the White Sox resurgence that began in the early '90s and culminated in a 2005 World Series crown. Dubbed "The Big Hurt" for his punishment of opposing pitchers, Thomas was arguably the greatest White Sox hitter ever. He set career club records in 11 offensive categories, including home runs, runs, total bases, and RBI. He relied not only on the strength of his hulking frame but also on a sharp eye and patience. Thomas spent most of 2005 on the disabled list, but it was fitting that he was part of the world championship team during his final Chicago season.

STATS

White Sox seasons: 1990–2005

Height: 6-foot-5

Weight: 250

- 5 seasons with 40 or more HR
- .301 career BA
- 2-time AL MVP
- 5-time All-Star

FRANK THOMAS
FIRST BASEMAN

CHICAGO
WHITE SOX

SHADOW OF THE BLACK SOX

Soon, however, the White Sox's lack of offense would prove too much to overcome. Walsh won 40 games in 1908, but an anemic offense produced only 3 home runs. The Sox sank in the standings until the roster was rebuilt starting around 1914. That year, pitcher Urban "Red" Faber—a spitballer known for his good control—came to town. Also new to the roster were right fielder "Shoeless Joe" Jackson, second baseman Eddie Collins, and pitcher Ed Cicotte.

The Sox reached the World Series in 1917 after a 100–54 season, then topped the New York Giants to win the championship. They roared back to the World Series two years later but were upset by the Cincinnati Reds in eight games (in an experimental, best-of-nine series). A year later, it would come to light that eight of Chicago's players had thrown the series, or lost on purpose in exchange for money. The scandal left a lasting mark on professional baseball,

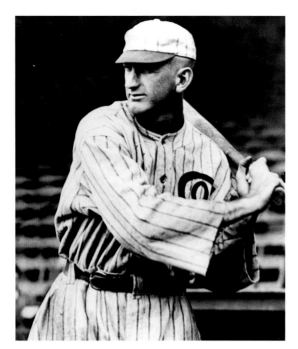

and the eight would go down in history as the "Black Sox" for their misdeed.

In 1920, the White Sox were poised to take the AL pennant again. But when the Black Sox scandal surfaced, Chicago lost its winning edge and came in second to the Cleveland Indians. For the remainder of the decade, the Sox finished no better than fifth place. In fact, they wouldn't finish above third place for more than 30 years.

Throughout the 1930s, Sox fans gathered to cheer on such new stars as Luke Appling. The young shortstop joined Chicago in 1930 and steadily developed into an able fielder and one of the league's most consistent batsmen. He became an adroit slap hitter, taking advantage of outfield gaps in spacious Comiskey Park, the team's home stadium.

Appling and pitcher Ted Lyons faced the difficult task of leading the White Sox back to prominence—a feat they would never accomplish. In seven seasons during the 1930s, the White Sox finished with a losing record. One Sox player who seemed symbolic of the team in that era was first baseman Henry "Zeke" Bonura, who, in 1936, contributed 138

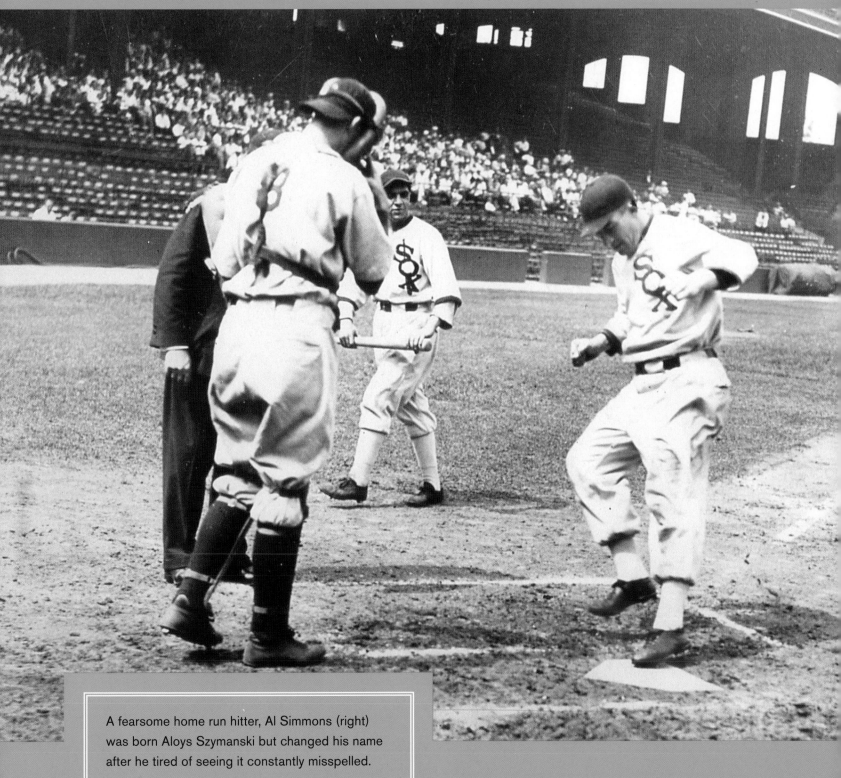

A fearsome home run hitter, Al Simmons (right) was born Aloys Szymanski but changed his name after he tired of seeing it constantly misspelled.

SECOND BASEMAN · EDDIE COLLINS

Eddie Collins began his professional baseball career while he was a junior at Columbia University. Although college athletes were not allowed to play pro sports, Collins used a fake name and joined the Philadelphia Athletics—until his true identity was discovered. Eventually, Collins became one of the greatest second basemen ever. His quickness made him one of the earliest elite base stealers, and at the plate, Collins had few peers, maintaining a .333 average over 25 big-league seasons. For 12 of those seasons, he played for Chicago, including the 1917 world championship squad and 1919 "Black Sox" team.

EDDIE COLLINS
SECOND BASEMAN

CHICAGO
WHITE SOX

STATS

White Sox seasons: 1915–26

Height: 5-foot-9

Weight: 175

- **.969 career fielding percentage**

- **1914 AL MVP**

- **741 career stolen bases**

- **Baseball Hall of Fame inductee (1939)**

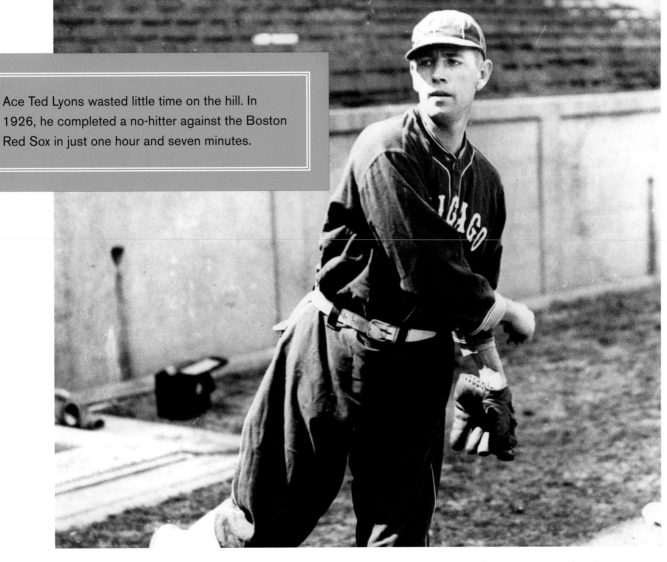

Ace Ted Lyons wasted little time on the hill. In 1926, he completed a no-hitter against the Boston Red Sox in just one hour and seven minutes.

runs batted in (RBI) at the plate but lacked zeal in the field. Bonura had a unique approach to fielding. If the ball looked too difficult to catch or scoop up, he watched it go by. One year, he avoided tough plays so fervently that he actually led the league in fielding percentage.

By 1938, Chicago sat in the AL cellar. Things didn't get much better during the 1940s, as the Sox produced only two winning seasons during the decade. "The whole White Sox squad is up for trade," manager Jimmy Dykes announced during one especially poor season. "We'll trade anybody, everybody . . . if we can."

WHITE SOX

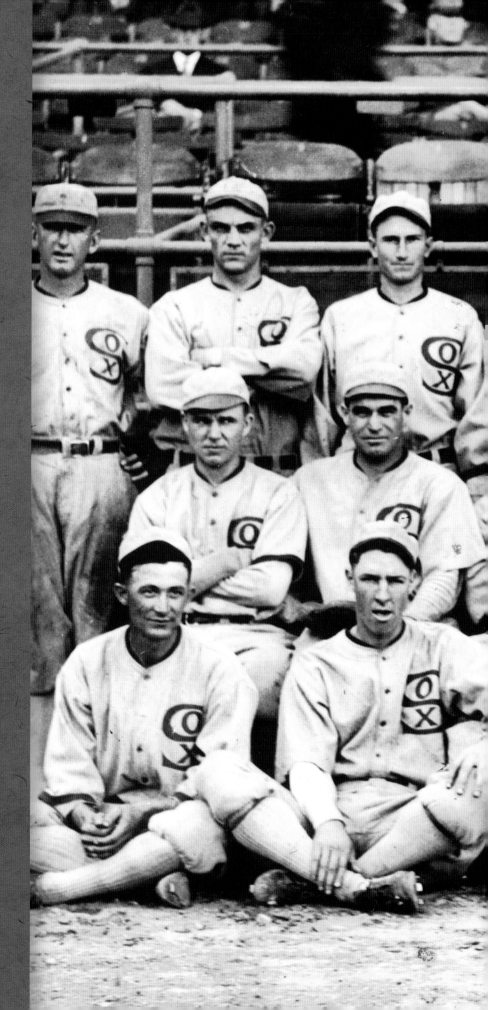

THE BLACK SOX SCANDAL

In Game 1 of the 1919 World Series, Chicago pitcher Ed Cicotte hit Cincinnati Reds second baseman Morrie Rath in the back with his second pitch of the game. Cicotte, a 29-game winner, had hit only 2 batters all season. Few knew it yet, but it was a signal: the fix was in. The White Sox were heavily favored to beat the Reds, yet as the first game neared, rumors circulated that gamblers had paid a number of Chicago's players to let Cincinnati win. Cicotte's beaning of Rath let the gamblers know that the players had agreed to split the $100,000 bribe. The "throw" was subtle—consisting of wild pitches, fielding errors, strikeouts, and a lack of hustle—and despite the rumors, no one was sure if the Sox had intentionally lost or if the Reds had simply been the better team. But in September 1920, pressured by investigators, Cicotte and outfielder Joe Jackson confessed. The eight players involved—Cicotte, Jackson, pitcher Lefty Williams, outfielder Happy Felsch, third baseman Buck Weaver, first baseman Chick Gandil, shortstop Swede Risberg, and third baseman Fred McMullin—were banned from baseball for life and became known as the Chicago "Black Sox."

1919 WHITE SOX

THE SOX GET GO-GOING

he White Sox of the 1950s were known as the "Go-Go Sox" for their speed on the base paths and their hustle on defense. The team led the AL in stolen bases for 11 straight seasons starting in 1951. But the nickname could just as easily have come from the way the team was built. Under the direction of new general manager Frank "Trader" Lane, players came and went so rapidly that the team that started the 1951 season featured not a single player from the 1949 squad.

One noteworthy addition was second baseman Jacob "Nellie" Fox, who arrived in 1950 and played for the Sox until 1963, leading the AL in hits four times and winning a league Most Valuable Player (MVP) award along the way. Fox was one of baseball's all-time steadiest players. He almost never struck out, held the major-league fielding percentage record in his day, and once played 798 consecutive games at second base.

Left fielder Orestes "Minnie" Minoso joined the team in 1951. Minoso was the first African American player to suit up for Chicago and quickly became a White Sox fan favorite due to his enthusiastic play. Still,

THIRD BASEMAN · ROBIN VENTURA

Robin Ventura came to the major leagues with big expectations after a stellar college career at Oklahoma State University and a stint with the 1988 U.S. Olympic team. Ventura met those expectations and then some. He played 10 of his 16 major-league seasons with the White Sox and built a career on strong all-around play. He manned the "hot corner" with a sure glove, quick reflexes, and a strong arm. At the plate, his strength was driving runners home. In 1991, he knocked in 100 runs for the White Sox, and in 1996, he drove in 105.

ROBIN VENTURA
THIRD BASEMAN

CHICAGO
WHITE SOX

STATS

White Sox seasons: 1989–98

Height: 6-foot-1

Weight: 198

- *Baseball America*'s **College Player of the Decade (1980s)**

- **1,182 career RBI**

- **6-time Gold Glove winner**

- **2 grand slams in a single game (1995)**

COMISKEY PARK

In 1908, White Sox owner Charlie Comiskey bought 15 acres of land at the corner of 35th Street and Shields Avenue on Chicago's working-class South Side. Two years later, Comiskey Park, a $500,000 concrete-and-steel stadium with seating for 35,000, was complete. The outfield stretched 420 feet deep to center and 362 feet down the lines. The first game was played there on July 1, 1910, against the St. Louis Browns. In July 1933, Major League Baseball's first All-Star Game was played there. Chicago outfielder Al Simmons and third baseman Jimmy Dykes played in that game, along with such baseball legends as Babe Ruth, Jimmie Foxx, and Lefty Grove. Comiskey also hosted All-Star Games in 1950 and 1984. And from 1933 to 1950, the Negro League All-Star Game was played there as well. On September 30, 1990, when the last game was played at Comiskey Park, it was the oldest stadium in use—older than Boston's Fenway Park and Chicago's Wrigley Field. A new Comiskey Park was built directly across the road, and for a time, before old Comiskey was torn down, a person could stroll down 35th Street between the old Comiskey and the new. In 2003, the ballpark was renamed U.S. Cellular Field.

there were some who did not appreciate Minoso's presence. In 1953, he and African American pitcher Connie Johnson were forced to skip an exhibition game in Memphis, Tennessee, because a town ordinance prohibited blacks and whites from playing together on the local field.

Another player who got the Sox of the '50s going was center fielder "Jungle" Jim Rivera, who was known for his belly-flopping slides and wild personality. Rivera once dove head first into home plate—after slugging a home run into the outfield seats. When he emerged from the dust, he asked the photographers in attendance if they got their shot.

Pitcher Billy Pierce, meanwhile, led Chicago's efforts on the mound. With a hard fastball and a sharp, darting slider, Pierce relentlessly whipped balls past helpless hitters. Lane once said of the Go-Go's ace, "You didn't need a relief pitcher when he pitched. If he had a one-run lead going into the seventh or eighth inning, the ballgame was over."

With this hard-charging style of play, Chicago finally started winning. But after finishing third behind the New York Yankees and Cleveland Indians for five straight years, the Sox knew they still lacked pieces to the pennant puzzle. In 1957, they lured manager Al Lopez away from the

Indians. They also added speedy outfielder Jim Landis and speedier shortstop Luis Aparicio, who became the premier base stealer on a team of base stealers. Aparicio combined with Fox to create one of the most exciting middle-infield combinations in baseball.

Under Lopez's direction, the Sox rose to second place in 1957 and 1958. Then, in 1959, led by hard-throwing pitcher Early Wynn, the Sox took over first place in July and never gave it up. On September 22, the White Sox clinched their first pennant in 40 years—the first since the 1919 Black Sox had won it.

This time, Chicago gave its all in the World Series. Fox batted .375, while big first baseman Ted Kluszewski drove in 10 runs. The White Sox rolled to victory in Game 1 but could not get past the Los Angeles Dodgers, losing the series four games to two. "When we won the first game 11–0, I figured, 'Boy, this is going to be it,'" Pierce said later. "It didn't turn out that way, but I still think we had a great ballclub." The White Sox would have to wait another 40-plus years to reach the World Series again.

WHITE SOX

TED KLUSZEWSKI

A 6-foot-2 and 230-pound slugger, Ted Kluszewski cut the sleeves off his jersey, which served to both liberate his swing and show off his biceps.

SHORTSTOP · LUKE APPLING

Luke Appling was famous for his ability to foul off pitch after pitch until he got one he liked. He once smacked away 17 foul balls in a single at bat before ripping a triple. Appling approached his career much the same way. Although he never won a pennant with the luckless White Sox, he played all 20 of his big-league seasons with the team, perhaps waiting for the big season that never came. Even as his long career drew to an end, Appling's hitting prowess barely diminished. In 1949, his 19th season, the 42-year-old hit .301 with 121 walks.

LUKE APPLING
SHORTSTOP

CHICAGO
WHITE SOX

STATS

White Sox seasons: 1930–43, 1945–50

Height: 5-foot-10

Weight: 183

- 7-time All-Star

- 2-time AL leader in BA

- .310 career BA

- Baseball Hall of Fame inductee (1964)

NORTH AND SOUTH

or the next three decades, the White Sox would go "north and south" frequently—not on the map but in the standings. The Sox played some exciting baseball but lacked consistency from year to year. Unlike the Go-Go Sox teams, which progressed steadily to the top of the league, the Sox of the 1960s, '70s, and '80s often found themselves in second place one season and near the AL basement the next.

Following the successful 1959 season, the Sox floundered, dropping to fifth place by 1962. Again, a new squad was assembled, this one featuring pitchers Gary Peters and Hoyt Wilhelm. Peters, a starter, won a total of 39 games in 1963 and 1964. Wilhelm, meanwhile, made 98 saves for Chicago in a bullpen role on his way to the Baseball Hall of Fame.

The 1964 White Sox finished the season with nine straight victories but fell one game short of the AL pennant. After another strong finish in 1965, they steadily declined, dropping to eighth place by 1968. Then, the 1970 White Sox team made a southward plunge like no other. They

LEFT FIELDER · MINNIE MINOSO

Saturnino Orestes Armas "Minnie" Minoso was born in Cuba. At age 14, he quit school to work in the local sugar cane fields and eventually started a plantation ballclub, and his skills earned him a trip to Havana to play for the semipro Cuba Mining Company team. He later joined the New York Cubans, the Cleveland Indians, and, finally, the Chicago White Sox.

Minoso was a fan favorite due to his hustle and enthusiasm as a leader of the "Go-Go Sox." Sadly, Minoso was not on Chicago's pennant-winning 1959 team, as he was part of the 1958 trade that brought pitching ace Early Wynn to Chicago.

MINNIE MINOSO
LEFT FIELDER

CHICAGO
WHITE SOX

STATS

White Sox seasons: 1951–57, 1960–61, 1964, 1976, 1980

Height: 5-foot-10

Weight: 175

- .298 career BA

- 7-time All-Star

- 3-time AL leader in stolen bases

- 3-time Gold Glove winner

A RECORD-BREAKING PROMOTION

To help attract fans to a July 12, 1979, doubleheader between the White Sox and the Detroit Tigers at Chicago's Comiskey Park—and to kill the worn-out musical genre of disco once and for all—Sox owner Bill Veeck, his son Mike, and a Chicago radio disc jockey named Steve Dahl collaborated to create a promotion called "Disco Demolition Night." Fans donating disco records could buy tickets at a deep discount, and between the two games, the records would be placed in a large wooden crate on the field and blown up. The promotion quickly went awry when the first game (a 4–1 Tigers win) was repeatedly disrupted by fans in the sold-out stadium who flung records onto the field like Frisbees. When the army-helmet-wearing Dahl oversaw the records demolition between games, a fire—and then pandemonium—broke out, with an estimated 7,000 mutinous fans storming the field. Eventually, the Chicago riot police were brought in to quell the uprising. But due to the scorched and torn-up field and wild atmosphere, the umpires called the game off, and the Sox were forced to forfeit. "We have found a lot of ways to lose games this year," said Sox skipper Don Kessinger, "but I guess we've added a new wrinkle."

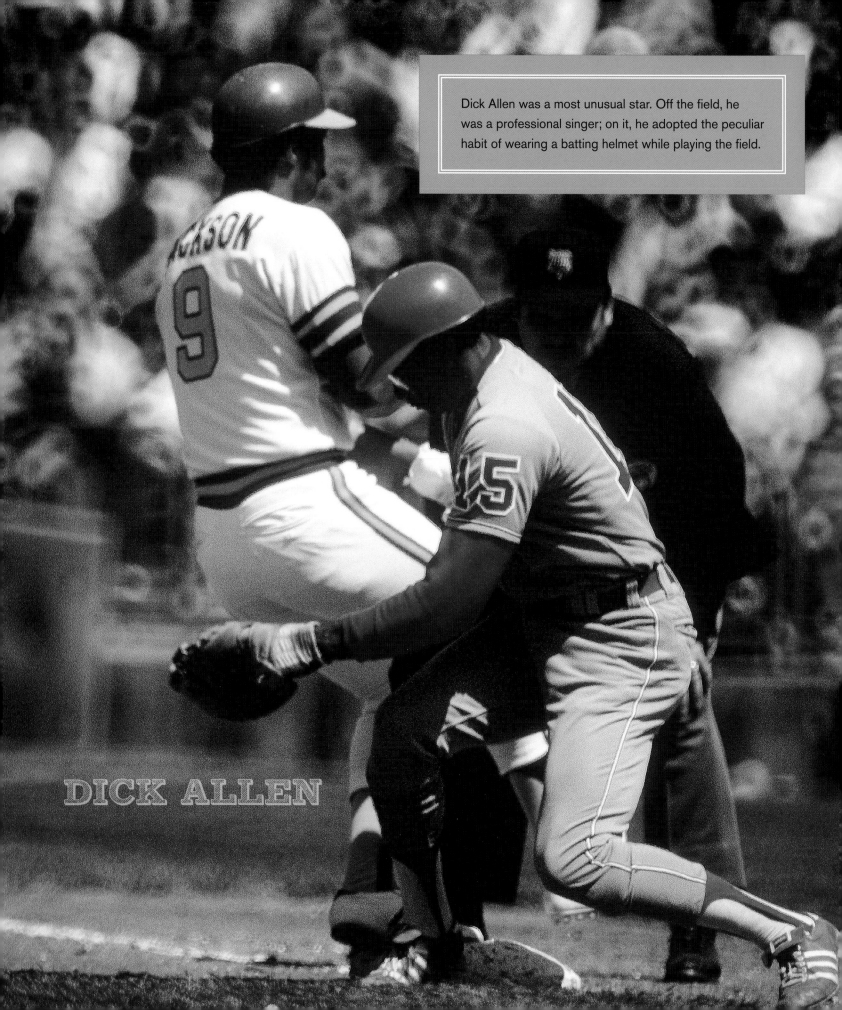

Dick Allen was a most unusual star. Off the field, he was a professional singer; on it, he adopted the peculiar habit of wearing a batting helmet while playing the field.

DICK ALLEN

lost 106 games, a club record, and finished a whopping 42 games behind the first-place Minnesota Twins.

Although the White Sox continued to struggle throughout the 1970s, they had some talent in the lineup. First baseman Dick "Richie" Allen led the AL with 37 home runs and 113 RBI to win the 1972 MVP award. Allen had joined the team after tumultuous seasons with the Philadelphia Phillies and St. Louis Cardinals. The first baseman was famous for his surliness, but he was an immensely powerful hitter whose blasts sometimes cleared the outfield stands entirely. "Now I know why they boo Richie all the time," joked Pittsburgh Pirates first baseman Willie Stargell. "When he hits a home run, there's no souvenir." Unfortunately for the White Sox, the moody Allen quit the team with one month left in the 1974 season, despite leading the AL in homers at the time.

Allen's decision baffled teammates and fans. Luckily for the White Sox, though, Wilbur Wood's knuckleballs baffled Chicago's opponents. The left-handed Wood won 90 games between 1971 and 1974. A few years after that, designated hitter Oscar Gamble put together a stellar season as part of a 1977 Sox team that became known as the "South-Side Hitmen." The Hitmen slugged 192 home runs, the most ever by a White Sox team. Gamble led the charge with 31 dingers, and outfielder Richie Zisk slammed 30 of his own. The team finished in third place but kept the fans' attention, drawing a team-record 1,657,135 spectators to Comiskey Park.

In 1983, the Sox jumped into first place in the AL Western Division (the league had been split into two divisions in 1969) and drew more than two million fans. That team featured hard-nosed catcher Carlton Fisk, ace pitcher LaMarr Hoyt, and clutch-hitting outfielder Harold Baines. The top overall selection in Major League Baseball's 1977 draft, Baines had been scouted by the White Sox since he was a Little-Leaguer and would play a total of 14 seasons in Chicago.

The 1983 Sox finished with 99 victories, the most since their 1917 world title-winning season, and faced the Baltimore Orioles in the AL Championship Series (ALCS). They lost, three games to one, and never found such success again for the rest of the 1980s. Chicago would finish near the bottom of the league standings the rest of the decade.

If the White Sox of the 1960s, '70s, and '80s shifted unpredictably like a knuckleball, the Sox of the '90s and 2000s sped upward like a hard-rising fastball. In 1990, a youthful Chicago squad took the field, led by enormous first baseman Frank Thomas, dependable third baseman

CENTER FIELDER · JIM LANDIS

Jim Landis roamed Comiskey Park's center field with speed and grace for eight seasons. New York Yankees manager Casey Stengel once commented that Landis's defense cut triples down to doubles and doubles down to singles. The sure-gloved Landis positioned himself well, got good jumps on fly balls, and made strong throws. And while not known for his hitting, he did many little things right at the plate. He averaged 60 walks a season for Chicago, was a capable base stealer, and in 1959 led the AL in sacrifices—bunts and fly outs that moved runners to the next base.

JIM LANDIS
CENTER FIELDER

CHICAGO
WHITE SOX

STATS

White Sox seasons: 1957–64

Height: 6-foot-1

Weight: 180

- **1962 All-Star**

- **5-time Gold Glove winner**

- **.989 career fielding percentage**

- **50 career triples**

Robin Ventura, and fiery pitcher Jack McDowell. The team boasted speed, defense, power, enthusiasm—and some of the league's best pure talent. In 1993, Thomas won the AL MVP award, and McDowell won the Cy Young Award as the league's best pitcher. That season, Chicago reached the playoffs for the first time in 10 years. The young Sox met the veteran Toronto Blue Jays in the ALCS. Chicago battled hard, erasing a two-games-to-none deficit with a pair of victories in Toronto. But McDowell never found his best stuff, and the Sox never won a third game. The Jays took the pennant and went on to win their second straight world championship.

Chicago came back strong the next year, charging to a 67–46 mark, but a players' strike then cut the season short and cancelled the 1994 World Series. The disruption seemed to hurt Chicago's momentum, and the Sox—though still formidable—would climb no higher than second place in the newly formed AL Central Division for the remainder of the decade.

At the start of the new millennium, the White Sox emerged as an offensive machine led by Thomas and slugging right fielder Magglio

Jack McDowell's stardom in Chicago was intense but fleeting, as he posted win totals of 17, 20, and 22 from 1991 to 1993 but then faded.

Ordoñez. During the 2000 season, 5 players scored more than 100 runs, 4 players batted over .300, 5 players knocked in more than 90 runs, and the Sox led the AL in runs scored. It was a slugfest all season long as the Sox rolled to an AL-best 95 victories. Excitement in the Windy City came to a screeching halt, though, as the Sox were swept by the Seattle Mariners in three tight playoff games.

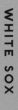

WHITE SOX

WINNING UGLY

The 1983 White Sox got off to a slow start. Near the end of May, their record was a mere 16–24, and at the midseason All-Star Game break, they were just 40–37. Fortunately for the Sox, no team was dominating Chicago's division, the AL West. The Texas Rangers led at the break with a 44–34 record, three and a half games ahead of the Sox. But as Chicago began to pick up steam, Rangers manager Doug Rader was quoted in a Dallas newspaper as saying that the Sox weren't for real. "Their bubble has got to burst," he said. "They're not playing that well. They're winning ugly." The Sox used Rader's quote as fuel for their charge to the playoffs. "Winning ugly" became the team's battle cry for the rest of the season, which the White Sox dominated. They went on six winning streaks of four games or more—the longest being an eight-game tear in early September. Chicago pummeled opponents that last stretch of the season, collecting nearly half of its AL-best 99 victories in August and September. By the end of the year, the Sox were in the playoffs for the first time in 24 years, finishing an astonishing 22 games ahead of the third-place Rangers.

RIGHT FIELDER · JOE JACKSON

"Shoeless Joe" Jackson's 13th major-league season was an unlucky one, as he was barred from major league baseball for his role in throwing the 1919 World Series. But that stretch of 13 seasons was anything but unlucky for Shoeless Joe. A natural ballplayer, Jackson was a swift, strong-throwing outfielder and such a pure hitter that the legendary Babe Ruth is said to have studied and mimicked Jackson's batting stance. With a lifetime .356 average, Shoeless Joe may have been the best hitter never to win a batting title. During the 1919 World Series that Jackson supposedly threw, he batted .375 with six RBI.

JOE JACKSON
RIGHT FIELDER

CHICAGO
WHITE SOX

STATS

White Sox seasons: 1915–20

Height: 6-foot-1

Weight: 200

- **2-time AL leader in hits**
- **168 career triples**
- **1,772 career hits**
- **Career-high .408 BA in 1911**

MANAGER · AL LOPEZ

As a player in the 1930s and '40s, Al Lopez was a catcher with a gift for handling pitchers. It was a gift that served him well when he moved into the managerial ranks. Lopez was not only skilled at handling players but also at making the most of their unique skills. As a coach for the Cleveland Indians, Lopez relied on power hitting and pitching. But when he became the White Sox's skipper in 1957, he preached a speed game that suited Comiskey's deep outfield and his players' natural abilities. Lopez engineered the "Go-Go Sox" and Chicago's first pennant in 40 years.

AL LOPEZ
MANAGER

CHICAGO
WHITE SOX

STATS

White Sox seasons as manager:
   1957–65, 1968–69

Managerial record: 1,410–1,004

AL pennant: 1959

Baseball Hall of Fame inductee
   (1977)

RETURN TO GLORY

The Sox hovered near the top of the AL Central for the next four years, and when they finally returned to the postseason in 2005, it was in surprising fashion. No player batted .300, no pitcher won 20 games, and only 1 player—first baseman Paul Konerko—knocked in 100 runs. Few people expected the White Sox to make the playoffs, even after the team got off to a blazing 24–7 start.

Former Sox shortstop-turned-manager Ozzie Guillen lit a fire under his squad and engineered a "small-ball" strategy that involved moving runners home one base at a time. Outstanding defense by such players as catcher A. J. Pierzynski and a strong pitching staff led by Jon Garland kept Chicago in close games all year. The Sox slumped badly at the start of August, and the Indians seemed poised to overtake them. But Chicago then caught a second wind and blew through the end of its schedule, sweeping the Indians in the season's final three games to win the division 99–63.

From then on, the Sox were simply unstoppable. In the face of an 88-year world championship drought, and still in the far-reaching shadow of the Black Sox scandal, Chicago dominated the postseason, winning an incredible 11 of 12 games. Third baseman Joe Crede and outfielder Jermaine Dye starred as Chicago mowed down the Boston Red Sox, Los Angeles Angels of Anaheim, and Houston Astros to become world champions. "It means a lot not only to us in the clubhouse but to the organization, to the fans, to the city, and it's just a great feeling," said Dye.

Chicago's title defense fell short in 2006 when, despite a fine 90–72 season, the White Sox finished in third place behind the Twins and Tigers in the AL Central. But the 2008 Sox found some magic again. Holdovers from the club's 2005 championship team joined with new veteran acquisitions such as first baseman Jim Thome and outfielder Ken Griffey Jr., as well as budding stars such as shortstop Alexei Ramirez and left fielder Carlos Quentin. Chicago enjoyed first-place status in the division much of the season until the Twins tied them at the campaign's very end, resulting in a one-game playoff.

In a game to remember at a chilly U.S. Cellular Field (the Sox's home since 1991), starting Sox pitcher John Danks threw a masterful eight innings of two-hit ball against the Twins. In the fifth inning, Griffey

GEOFF BLUM

A MARATHON MATCHUP

Game 3 of the 2005 World Series between the White Sox and the Houston Astros was long. How long? The longest World Series game ever—5 hours and 41 minutes long, 14 innings long, 482 pitches long. Chicago's leadoff hitter, outfielder Scott Podsednik, had a record eight at bats. The White Sox and Astros used a record 17 pitchers between them, and the 2 teams combined for 21 walks, used 43 players, and stranded 30 base runners—all World Series records. But the record that counted most to Chicago fans was the one when the game was done. In the top of the 14th inning, Chicago second baseman Geoff Blum—in his first World Series at bat—cranked a two-out homer down the right-field line of Houston's Minute Maid Park. The Sox scored one insurance run and then held off the Astros, who put runners on first and third base in the bottom half of the inning but failed to score. When the marathon game finally ended, the White Sox found themselves with a 7–5 victory and a three-games-to-none lead in the series. One night later, they would celebrate the team's first world championship in 88 years—ending a drought that was also a record.

GORDON BECKHAM

Rookie Gordon Beckham opened eyes around the AL in 2009 by posting 14 home runs with 63 RBI while playing in only 103 games.

Brian Anderson's memorable catch versus the Twins at the end of the 2008 campaign sealed Chicago's second AL Central title in four seasons.

denied the Twins' best shot at a score with a beautiful throw to Pierzynski that cut down a Minnesota base runner trying to score on a sacrifice fly. "That play, all I had to do was make a good throw," said Griffey. "The credit is all A. J. I put a two-hopper in there, and he was able to get it and block the plate." In the seventh, Thome staked the home team to a 1–0 lead with a solo home run blast. Reliever Bobby Jenks then came in and closed the game in the ninth, with the final out being recorded when center fielder Brian Anderson made a spectacular diving catch.

Although the White Sox fell to the upstart Tampa Bay Rays in the 2008 AL Division Series (ALDS), losing three games to one, Chicago remained a contender in the seasons that followed. In 2009, the Sox came up short of the postseason, but infielder Gordon Beckham emerged as a young star, and pitcher Mark Buehrle threw a gem for the record books—a perfect game versus the Rays. For his efforts, Buehrle

MARK BUEHRLE

President Obama and the rest of the White Sox faithful hoped that pitcher Mark Buehrle would lead the South-Siders back to the playoffs in 2011.

received a congratulatory phone call from U.S. president Barack Obama, a Chicago native and longtime Sox loyalist. The White Sox missed the postseason again in 2010, despite Konerko slugging 39 home runs and outfielder Juan Pierre swiping an AL-high 68 bases.

In more than 11 decades of play, the White Sox have given fans heroes and stories worth rooting for throughout the late springs, summers, and early autumns of Chicago's South Side. They have also given the Windy City three unforgettable world championships. Fans of Chicago's beloved "Pale Hose" can't wait for the day when the winds of fortune blow a fourth title their way.

INDEX